V-C

10/83

DISCARD

EVERYDAY PRAYERS

For All Sorts of Needs

Wallace Fridy

Abingdon Press

Nashville   New York

EVERYDAY PRAYERS

Library of Congress Cataloging in Publication Data

FRIDY, WALLACE.
    Everyday prayers for all sorts of needs.
    1. Prayers. I. Title.
BV245.F695   242'.8   73-14745

ISBN 0-687-12332-1

MANUFACTURED BY THE PARTHENON PRESS AT
NASHVILLE, TENNESSEE, UNITED STATES OF AMERICA

Foreword

In its broadest sense, prayer is an act of worship; in its narrowest sense, it is an appeal for some special benefit. In the first sense courage can be prayer, and silence; humility, and generosity. In short, whatever dignifies and glorifies human nature, and as a result praises God, is prayer.

But in the ordinary meaning of the term, prayer is coming to God with our memories, our hopes, our tears, our thanksgivings. The custom is an ancient, a noble, and a most reasonable one. As Tennyson reminds us, if we did not lift our hands in prayer, we should be no better than the animals.

This approach to God should be, I think, in noble thought clothed in befitting language. As would be natural to expect, too many spontaneous or impromptu prayers are lacking in both thought and expression.

It has been a privilege and a revelation for me to read this most admirable book of prayers by Dr. Wallace Fridy. His prayers have originality, spiritual depth, and great clarity and felicity of expression. It is with a sense of gratitude for what they have done for me that I recommend them to others.

—*Archibald Rutledge*

Contents

Morning

A Morning Prayer

O God, for another day, for another morning, for another hour, for another minute, for another chance to live and serve thee, I am truly grateful. Do thou this day free me—
   From fear of the future;
   From anxiety for the morrow;
   From bitterness toward anyone;
   From cowardice in face of danger;
   From laziness in face of work;
   From failure before opportunity;
   From weakness when thy power is at hand.
But fill me with—
   Love that knows no barrier;
   Courage that cannot be shaken;
   Faith strong enough for the darkness;
   Strength sufficient for my tasks;
   Loyalty to thy kingdom's goal;
   Wisdom to meet life's complexities;
   Power to lift men unto thee.
Be thou with me for another day and use me as thou wilt; in Christ's name I pray. AMEN.

Facing a New Day

O God, as the shades of night are lifted and the glow of the eastern sky pushes back the darkness announcing the dawn, so do thou enter the recesses of our hearts and bring light to the clouded parts. Gracious One, through this new day help us—

To be diligent in use of time;

To be faithful to every trust;

To be extravagant in thy service;

To be watchful of words we utter;

To be generous in our criticism of others;

To be courageous in time of testing;

To be aware of the needs of men;

To be slow to expose;

To be quick to believe the best;

To be responsive to thy voice;

To be dependent upon thy strength;

To be accompanied by thy presence;

Through Jesus Christ our Lord. AMEN.

Rejoicing in the Day

Holy, holy, holy, Lord God Almighty, heaven and earth are full of thy glory; glory be to thee, O Lord most high. Help us, our Father, to rejoice today in thy worship and find gladness in the singing of thy praises.

Enable us to step aside from the busy life of common days and take thought of life's meaning and its end.

We would remember our loved ones in far-off places. Guard and protect them, we pray.

Forgive us for our failures of the past, and strengthen us for our opportunities of the future, through Jesus Christ our Lord. AMEN.

In Gratitude for This Day

O God, we would know thee today, for this is the day that thou hast made. Help us to be joyous in it. Consecrate the experience of this day to thy service.

Grant that we may be kinder in our homes, more considerate in our business relationships, and more devoted to thy church. Help us to walk daily without fear, but with trust. Help us to follow the light of thy truth in dark places and to do right when it is so easy to do wrong.

Forgive us for our low moods when we should be joyous. Forgive us for the little sins which lay waste life when thy strength can enable us to overcome them. Control our pride which separates us from thee, and grant that the misfortunes which come our way will lead us back to thee, through Jesus Christ our Lord. AMEN.

For the Beauty of the Day

O Thou eternal God, who art beyond the reach of our highest thoughts, and yet who art within each one of us, we come before thee this day praising thy holy name.

On every hand we see thy handiwork—in the beauty of this day, in the joys of earthly companionship, in the laughter of little children, in the affection we have for one another. But especially, our Father, we see thee and know thee in Jesus Christ our Lord. We remember his words, "He that hath seen me hath seen the Father." Help us to be more like him, to see in him the kind of person thou wouldst have us be. Give to us the consciousness of thy Holy Spirit which guides us and upholds us.

Send us forth to live at our best, through Jesus Christ our Lord. Amen.

As We Begin the Day

Eternal God, thou who art the light of the minds that know thee, the strength of the wills that serve thee, and the life of the souls that love thee, help us so to know thee that we may truly love thee, and so to love thee that we may fully serve thee, whom to serve is perfect freedom.

Grant that we may fashion our lives according to thy will and purpose. O God, we are wearied with the demands made upon us, the tasks our hands have had to do, the temptations which confront us, the decisions which claim our attention, the rush and hurry of daily life; all these have taken heavy toll upon our spirits.

We pray that this will be an hour of renewal, that we may find here water from an everflowing spring that will quench our thirst, food from thy boundless storehouse that will nourish our spirits, and light from thy limitless wisdom that will illumine our pathway. In the name and in the spirit of Christ we pray. AMEN.

For Power to Do God's Will

O Lord, thou who hast given us another day to serve thee, we lift our hearts in humble gratitude. Our souls do thirst for thee, O God, the living God. Our hearts are restless until they find their rest in thee. In quietness and in confidence thou dost give that rest.

Touch us this day, O God, where our need is greatest. To those in despair, grant new hope; to those bound down with sin, give freedom of release; to those faced with personal failure, grant the courage to start over again; to those faced with illness, help them to know thy comfort; to those for whom life has become meaningless, give that joy which is the portion of those who follow thee. In Jesus' name we pray. AMEN.

For New Life Every Day

Eternal God, thou who hast made us and who dost care for us, we thank thee for this thy world—our dwelling place. Thou hast richly furnished it for our use.

We are grateful for new life which greets us every day, for the stirring of nature from winter's sleep, for the soil and sunshine, for floating clouds and the rain, for the beauty of thy earth.

We thank thee, not only for life's joys and pleasures, but for thy presence and care in life's sorrows and suffering. We cannot explain why we are allowed to suffer, but we know that thou art good and that thou dost will for us the best. We are assured that underneath our lives are thy everlasting arms. Be especially near this day to all who lie on beds of pain. Sustain and strengthen them, we pray. Give to those who watch beside them—often in helpless waiting—thy assurance.

Grant that all of us may live so close to thee that when illness comes, we may be victorious sufferers, through Jesus Christ our Lord. AMEN.

For Confidence

O God our Father, we would quiet our souls in thy presence and rest ourselves in the confidence of thy sustaining strength.

We come before thee this day unworthy of thy love; we come stained by temptations which so easily beset us. We come feeling need of thee, thy power, thy strength, thy forgiveness. Thou knowest us better than we know ourselves. Take us this day and lift us upward. Strengthen our steps, enlarge our vision, quicken our hopes, purify our motives. Remind us of the things which do not change, and secure us to life's unfading treasures, through Jesus Christ our Lord. AMEN.

For a Closer Walk with God

O Thou, whose love has never let us go, and beyond whose brooding care we cannot drift; once more we lift our careworn hearts to thee. Here once again we bow before thee familiarly as child to parent, as friend to friend, seeking wisdom and hope, strength and courage. The day's toil is often too much for us:

> . . . late and soon
> Getting and spending, we lay waste our powers.

Breathe into our restless and disordered lives a portion of thy peace.

Through countless channels thou dost seek our lives, at many a door thou dost stand and knock, if we would but heed the accents of thy call. We wait now for thy still, small voice which can know that life's most important quest is finding thee and being found by thee, through Christ our Lord. AMEN.

For Mastery over Life's Details

O God, forgive us if the circumstances of life push us about, if details clog up our way and we fail to be their master, if the petty annoyances of everyday life mar our spirits. Let us not narrow our vision by the pressure of everyday routine, but rather do the tasks at hand in light of the larger goal ahead. Give to us the long view as we are forced to deal with the short view. Undergird us with a sense of the infinite as we face the finite duties of the hour. Strengthen us so that we are not driven by anxieties, fears, and unexpected interruptions, but drawn by love, goodwill, and truth. Give to us common sense in preserving our energies for tasks that mean most to thy kingdom; in the name of Christ, the supreme master of life, we pray. AMEN.

Night

For the Night

O God of the universe, creator of all life, companion of men's souls, for the night and all rest which it brings we are deeply grateful. We offer unto thee our labors for the day, regretting mistakes made but joyous for the privilege of serving thee. Grant us sleep which drives away the sorrows and burdens of our hearts and fits us again for work. As birds go to their nests, animals to their trees and holes, may we turn homeward grateful for the hours of darkness and the rest which they bring. For those who are sleepless, give them an abiding sense of thy presence and an assurance of thy care and protection. For those who toil while we sleep, grant unto them rest during daylight hours.

Drop thy still dews of quietness,
Till all our strivings cease;
Take from our souls the strain and stress,
And let our ordered lives confess
The beauty of thy peace.

AMEN.

To Be Not Afraid

Eternal God, thou hast been our dwelling place in all generations; thou art our refuge and strength. With grateful hearts we praise thee this day.

We thank thee for thy watchful care during the darkness of the night. We know that thou art ever near to guide and to guard. Even when we are unaware of it, thy love reaches out to us and blesses us.

Here this day we rest our fears in thy keeping, and we are not afraid of what life may bring to us. With thee as our companion and friend, we know that we are never alone.

But we do confess that at times we lose the consciousness of thy presence and wander far from home. At times we question whether life is worth living, and yet in our better moments we know that it is—when we follow thy way. Help us know that thou art always waiting to receive us back again. When we are bewildered by decisions which are hard to make, be for us a light unto our path, for we need thy wisdom here.

Give us this day a clearer grasp of the things which belong unto our peace and a closer walk with him who is the source of our peace. Through Jesus Christ our Lord we pray. AMEN.

Grateful for the Day

O God, grant that we may not begrudge time spent in thy presence, for it is in such moments that our eyes are made to see and our ears to hear. Thou art so good to us, O God. All that we have—life, health, home, church, work, friends, food—cometh from thy hand.

Let us not go through another day without acknowledging our debt; let us not have any success which would cause us to forget our dependence; let us take what has been given and give it back unto thee. O God, help us to be generous in our opinions of others, considerate of all we meet, patient with those with whom we work, diligent in our study, faithful to every trust, courageous in the face of danger, humble in all our living, prayerful every hour, joyous in all life's experiences, and free from all that would shut thee out. Through Jesus Christ our Lord we pray. AMEN.

In Gratitude for God's Presence

Eternal God, in whom there is no darkness, and from whom we find light for life's journey, thou art great in power, unlimited in wisdom, and infinite in all the resources of thy being.

Through countless channels thou dost seek our lives; at many a door thou dost stand and knock. Help us to know that life's most important quest is finding thee and being found by thee. With gratitude we turn our thoughts toward thy mercy and love made known in so many ways. We know that thou art with us and blessing us even when we are unaware of thy presence. We are confident that thou dost will for our lives all that is good. We are assured through Christ our Lord that thou dost go with us in all life's experiences.

Help us to see with clearer eyes and keener vision that thou art the Way, the Truth, and the Life. Give to us the renewed conviction that life will work only as thou hast planned it, and as Christ hath made it known unto us. In his name we pray. AMEN.

In Praise and Thanksgiving

Eternal God, creator of all life, ruler of all nature, source of all strength, we praise thee, we glorify thee, we thank thee for thy great love toward us and all men. Into thy holy presence we come this day lifting our common supplications unto thee. Thou knowest the needs of our hearts; thou dost understand our fears and our unanswered perplexities. Meet us here this day, we pray.

But we would pray not only for ourselves and our need, but for others whose needs may be even greater than ours. For those brokenhearted through bereavement; disillusioned through disappointment; oppressed through hardship; burdened through a sense of guilt —be especially near to all these, we pray. Grant as thou dost brighten the world with sunshine that some beam of thy grace and hope will shine upon their disappointment and bring gladness and gratitude to their hearts. In Jesus' name we pray. AMEN.

A Prayer of Thanksgiving

O God, whose days are without end and whose mercies cannot be numbered, we lift our hearts in thanksgiving to thee. We thank thee for life, and the joy of it; for health, and all the powers with which thou hast endowed us; for family and friends, whose affection and love warm our hearts; and for thy companionship which guides our steps day by day.

Give us radiant spirits assured of thy love and mercy, confident that we cannot move beyond thy fatherly care. Thankful for the life thou hast given us, we ask thee to help us make the most of it. Help us to throw off the shackles of fear and anxiety, of gloom and depression, of pride and prejudice.

In our thanksgiving remind us of our dependence upon others and thee. In our sense of debt to the past, give us the incentive to glorify thee in the present by giving all that we are and have in thy service, through Jesus Christ our Lord. AMEN.

Praise and Thanksgiving

In Praise of God's Presence

O eternal One, whose majesty overwhelms us and
whose fatherly concern touches us—
    Without thee life is empty;
    Without thy power we fail in our own strength;
    Without thy care we could not live;
    Without thy forgiveness we perish through our
      sins;
    Without thy love, life holds no joy;
    Without thy presence we labor in vain;
    Without thy assurance life's fears stagger us;
    Without thy comfort life's tragedies overwhelm
      us;
    Without thy wisdom life holds no meaning;
    Without thy fatherly concern we tread the wine-
      press alone;
    Without thy strength we cannot bear the load;
    Without thee, O God, we fall by the wayside.
      But with a consciousness of thy abiding pres-
        ence,
      we carry on with courage,
      through Jesus Christ our Lord. AMEN.

In Praise of Jesus Christ

Almighty God, who hast caused the light of life to come forth out of darkness, with songs of joy and hearts filled with gratitude we pause in thy presence this day.

We thank thee for thy love which gave us Jesus Christ our Lord. We thank thee for his earthly life, for the temptations he faced, for his perfect manhood. We thank thee for his victory over death and for his sacrifices that we might know thy love and the saving power of his resurrection.

We thank thee that nothing can separate us from the love of Christ—tribulation, distress, persecution, famine, nakedness, peril, or sword. We are grateful to believe that thy love for us cannot be destroyed whatever we do. Help us, we pray, to accept ourselves and thy acceptance of us.

Meet us this day in the secret places of our souls. Walk through the hidden rooms of our hearts. Open the closets we have kept closed because of shame. Take from us all that is low and selfish, evil and of mean report, and lift up all that is beautiful and good, unselfish and of good report, through Jesus Christ our Lord. AMEN.

In Praise of God's Majesty

Eternal God, before whose majesty and power we stand in awe, and yet in whose presence we call thee Father, we raise to thee our grateful praise.

Through all the mystery of life help us to see behind it and in it a great God. In all the immensity of space and the unfathomable worlds about us, help us to affirm, like our fathers before us, "Before the mountains were brought forth, or ever thou hadst formed the earth and the world, from everlasting to everlasting thou art God."

Confront us, O God, with the truth that, in all the mystery of life and the immensity of space, we have a special place in thy concern.

Give us contrite hearts for our sins, and thankful hearts for thy forgiveness. Lure us toward the ideal of manhood thou hast set before us, but remind us that thou dost accept us as we are—imperfect children. In Christ's name we pray. AMEN.

In Praise of the Living Lord

O Thou eternal God, who hast made thyself known supremely in the coming of Jesus Christ our Lord; we rejoice that once again we may turn our eyes back to the event which has altered the course of history. We marvel at his birth, his teachings, but especially are we grateful for his presence here among us. We thank thee that thou didst send him as a Savior of mankind, a Redeemer who lifts us from our sins, and a companion who travels with us along life's dusty way.

Grant that he may become today the companion of our thoughts, so that his divine manhood may more and more take root within our souls. May the comfort of his presence bind up the wounds of the broken-hearted and give renewed hope to the grief-stricken.

Forgive us for our failures of the past and strengthen us for our opportunities of the future, through Jesus Christ our Lord we pray. AMEN.

For Knowledge of God

O Lord God, whose strength is sufficient for all who lay hold of it, and in whose power it is to give life and to recall life, we are grateful for this moment to praise and to worship thee. We thank thee that the slender threads of our being are now uncut, and still we can serve thee according to thy holy ways. Give us thankful hearts for life itself, and help us know that thou art the strength of our days as well as the source of our being.

Forgive us, O Lord, for our forgetfulness and negligence. We have too often forgotten thee in the mad rush to get ahead. We have sinned in thy sight, intent upon our own selfish ways. We have stayed too long in the marketplace and neglected the quiet place. We have paid homage to a world of things and ignored the spiritual world. We have lived too long in the glare of the streets, and need to pull apart that we may rightly see. Take us this day and make us aware of the spiritual world, through Jesus Christ our Lord. AMEN.

For a Sense of God's Presence

O gracious One, thou who dost continually reveal thyself to us, judge us not by our blindness which cannot see, but in thy understanding mercy. Help us to hear thy voice and see thee in life's common things. Everywhere dost thou loom up before us, if only we could see. In a blooming flower thy beauty is displayed; through rising and setting suns, lo thou art there; in the kindness of human hearts thou dost reside; even in sorrow and suffering can we find thee; in broken dreams and unfulfilled desires thou art there; here today in the quietness of this hour thy voice is speaking, thy strength and power are knocking at our doors. Do thou give us responsive hearts. Break down all prejudices and bitterness, all hatreds and evil will, which would shut thee out. Fill our being with love, courage, hope, faith, health, and send us out made-over in body, mind, and spirit, to live another day. In Christ's name we pray. AMEN.

In Thanksgiving for God's Provision

Most gracious Father, who art never far away from any of us and art found of them that diligently seek thee, we praise thee; we glorify thee; we give thanks unto thee for all thou art to us and all thou dost for us day by day.

Our hearts are filled with thanksgiving—

For life with all its joys and sorrows, the bitter mingled with the sweet;

For thy watchful care during hours of darkness;

For light of day and our privilege of working in it;

For food which fits us for labor and service;

For friends and loved ones who share life with us;

For a faith which undergirds and sustains in moments of darkness; and

For thy companionship always present to give us strength.

For all of these things we give thee our hearty thanks.

Speak to our special needs this day. Give to each of us a sure word, a comforting thought, renewed hope, undefeatable courage, through Jesus Christ our Lord. AMEN.

For Confidence in God

Eternal God, the ground of our being, the source of our strength, the center of our hope, the companion of our way, with gratitude on our lips and praise within our hearts, we laud and magnify thy holy name. Thou art in nature, yet greater than thy nature. Thou art in thy world, and yet greater than thy world. Thou art power, and yet more than power; mind, and yet more than mind; order, and yet more than order. Thou art love in all its deeper meanings. Our minds are too small to encompass thy nature, and our hearts are too feeble to experience thy fullness.

O God—

Keep us true;
Keep us faithful;
Keep us loving;
Keep us kind;
Keep us brave;
Keep us pure;
Keep us generous;
Keep us humble;
Keep us near.

In Jesus' name we pray. AMEN.

For God's Presence Through the Day

Eternal God, in whom we live and move and have our being, thou art our refuge and strength. With grateful hearts we praise thee this day. We know that thou art ever near to guard and to guide. Even when we are unaware of thy presence, thy love reaches out to us and blesses us.

Here this day we rest our fears into thy gracious keeping. We know that without thy strength life's loads would be too much for us and life's fears would cause us to stumble. Facing life with thee our moments of uncertainty turn to hours of adventure, and our times of suffering become opportunities for knowing thee better.

Give us this day a clearer grasp of the things which belong unto our peace, through Jesus Christ our Lord. AMEN.

For Courage and Hope

Eternal God, we are thankful that thou hast caused the light of life to come forth out of darkness, and that thou hast planted hope within our hearts.

In our satisfaction with mediocre living, we are grateful to turn to thee whose nature is perfection and whose way is unwavering for truth and righteousness. We are thankful that life will not work apart from thee, and that sooner or later we discover it. Be for us our guide when skies are blue as well as our protector in stormy weather. Steady us along life's pilgrimage and strengthen us in facing the tasks committed to our care.

Drive from our lives evil ways and make us over after the likeness of Christ our Lord, in whose name we pray. AMEN.

For the Consciousness of God's Presence

Eternal God, in whom our fathers trusted and in whom we trust, thou hast caused the light of eternal life to shine upon the world. Quicken in us, we beseech thee, the sense of thy gracious presence here this day.

We come with praise upon our lips and thanksgiving in our hearts. We thank thee for all prophetic spirits who have promised a better day and by their faith helped to usher it in. We thank thee for those men who through the centuries dared to believe in the coming of One who would share men's burdens and free men from sin. And now that he has come, grant us utter faith in him and make us more worthy servants of thine, through Jesus Christ our Lord. AMEN.

For Confident Hope

Eternal God, in whom we live and move and have our being, with grateful hearts we lift our prayers unto thee.

We thank thee for this lovely day and for every suggestion of thy presence in our midst. We are grateful for this hour of worship in which we may hear thy voice and feel thee near.

Give us a vision of life at its best. Lift us upward that we may see thy truth, and open our hearts that we may receive thy word. Be with all who are in distress this day—the sorrowful, the suffering, the overworked, the unemployed, the sinful, the sick, and the lost. Bring thy healing love to give release. Take from us despair and give us hope, through Jesus Christ our Lord. AMEN.

For God's Mercy

O God our Father, in whose hand our lives rest, and in whose providence we spend our days, there are so many mysteries that baffle our minds. There are so many questions we cannot answer. There are so many problems to make us doubt. We do not know and understand all we want to know. Our faith is not firm as we want it to be. But, O God, we do know enough of thy goodness, thy forgiveness, thy love, to make us want to hold fast to thee. We do know that—

Thou hast been so gracious and art one to whom we owe life itself;

Thy hand hath been upon our shoulders guiding faltering footsteps;

Thy presence hath surrounded our being, bringing comfort in hours of distress;

Thy love hath forgiven our sinful ways, offering new beginnings; and

Thy strength hath upheld us, reinforcing our weakness.

Continue, we pray, to illumine our darkness and displace our doubts with thy assurance. In his name, which is above all names, we pray. AMEN.

For New Life

Eternal God, whose greatness and majesty are beyond the reach of our highest thoughts, and yet who art within the heart of each one of us, we lift our voices in praise and adoration to thee. No interest of our lives escapes thy notice. No joy is foreign to thy understanding. No thought or motive is unknown to thee. Our lives stand before thee as open books. So, today we lay bare our hearts and minds asking that thou wilt cleanse them with thy goodness.

Into thy presence we come, conscious of our sins and shortcomings. So much have we done which we ought not to have done, and so much have we left undone that we ought to have done, that there is little health in us. But we come not as those who have no hope, nor as those who can only drown in their sins, for in thee do we find new life and forgiveness, new chances and beginnings. Take us as we are and make us over, we pray, through Jesus Christ our Lord. AMEN.

For Life in God

O God, we come to thee empty-handed, for all that we possess cometh from thee. We stand before thee as having nothing except what thou hast provided.

We are small, but thou art great;
We are weak, but thou art strong;
We are ignorant, but thou art wise;
We are finite, but thou are infinite;
We are revengeful, but thou art forgiving;
We are sinful, but thou art pure.

O God, how dependent we are upon thee. Thou art our hope, our strength, and our life. AMEN.

For Fellowship with God

Eternal God, in whom there is no darkness, and from whom we find light for life's journey, with gratitude we come into thy holy presence this day. We cannot fully know thee or completely understand thee; yet what we know inspires us to love and worship thee.

We rejoice that thou hast made thyself known to us through thy Son, Jesus Christ our Lord. Help us to find in him today, through the Holy Spirit, strength and power for our feeble lives. We rejoice that every event of our mortal lives is watched of thee. We know that nothing escapes thy notice. Renew within our hearts the faith that all things work together for good to them that love thee.

Grant to every one of us this day the help and strength we need. Fill our fearful lives with confident trust. Quicken our faltering steps to a steady pace. Flood our sorrowful hearts with abiding joy, and lift our lonely souls with thy comforting presence, through Christ our Lord. AMEN.

For the Beauty of the Earth

Almighty God, giver of every good and perfect gift, to thee we lift our praise and thanksgiving. On every hand we see thy mercy and love expressed. The world with all its bounty and loveliness is a creation of thy hand. Our lives with all their possibilities were fashioned by thee. Thou hast made it all and declared it good.

Whenever we see thy creation distorted we know it is partly man's sin which has caused it. Wherever men are in want it is not thy will, for there is enough and to spare in thy world. Wherever men are dying through mortal conflict thy will for them is being denied. Forgive us, O holy One, for our manifold sins. Judge us not according to our merits, but in thy great love and mercy toward us.

Send us forth to live at our best, through Jesus Christ our Lord. AMEN.

For Reassurance

O God our Father, once again we lift our voices unto thee in praise and adoration. Thou art beyond the reach of our minds and thoughts, and thy nature is too wonderful for us to comprehend; yet we know that thou art within the heart of each one of us. We marvel that thou art concerned in our little affairs. We rejoice to know that we can come to thee familiarly as child to parent, as friend to friend.

So, we pour out our hearts to thee. Our needs are many; our sins are manifold; our fears are crippling; our strength wanes when we need it most. Bring to us, we pray, a reassurance that all things work together for good to them that love thee. Remind us that, however far we may drift from the Father's house, the door of return is always open.

Renew within us a right spirit and a loving heart. Give to us strength to withstand life's temptations. Be with all for whom the light of day brings less joy than to ourselves—the suffering, the saddened, the lonely, the fearful, the guilty. Send us forth rejoicing in thy love and responding through our service, through Jesus Christ our Lord. AMEN.

For All Sorts of Needs

For All Sorts and Conditions of Men

Eternal God, who hast called us into life, and in whose hands our lives do rest, we offer to thee this day our praise and adoration. We come before thee asking that thou wilt push back the curtain of the spiritual world that we might get a glimpse of thee.

For all sorts and conditions of men we pray:

For those sick in body and disturbed in mind;

For those burdened with the guilt of sin;

For those living under oppression who know not freedom;

For all who labor on farms, that men may eat;

For all who patrol streets and fight fires, that men may be safe;

For all who serve their country, that it may remain free;

For all who labor as missionaries, that men may hear the Good News;

For all these, O God, we raise our petitions today.

Now we wait before thee, asking that Christ in all his courage, his steadfastness, his faith, his sympathy, his victorious power, may reach out to uphold us and to dwell within us. In his name we pray. AMEN.

46

For Diligent Use of Time

O Thou eternal One, who hast given us the raw materials out of which life is to be fashioned, who hast placed at our disposal all things needful in making life lovely, noble, beautiful, forgive us because we have misused thy bountiful gifts. We have misappropriated them for our own selfish gain. Our negligence has caused prized moments to slip from our use. Living in undisciplined ways has shattered much that could have been done in thy name. This day is far spent with little to show for its unredeemed hours. Grant, O gracious One, that of what remains it can partially be reclaimed. Drive us to accept life's demands in these remaining hours, that this day with all its privileges and opportunities will not be lost, through Jesus Christ our Lord. AMEN.

To Be Freed from Small Talk

O merciful God, forgive us for small talk: for talk—
   That is unkind about our neighbors;
   That is unbrotherly about our friends;
   That is untrue about our enemies;
   That is unbridled and can never be recalled;
   That is unchaste and defiles life's lovely ways;
   That is unmerciful toward others when thou art so merciful toward us.
But help us—
   To know that small talk is the product of empty minds;
   To drive from our consciousness meager thoughts, replacing them with eternal truths;
   To see within ourselves that which we dislike in others;
   To open our eyes to the beauty of life and man's goodness beneath his rough exterior;
   To "be kindly affectioned one to another with brotherly love"; and
   To "live peaceably with all men."
In the name of him who showed us how to love one another we pray. AMEN.

For Faith in Time of Trouble

O eternal One, we come again this day asking for thy ear and voice, and praying that thou wilt listen to what we have to say and speak to us what thou wouldst have us know. Thou hast spoken to us in sorrow and in joy; in the watches of the night and at noonday; when the clouds were hanging low and when the sun had swept them away. Help us, we pray, to hold steady even when all sense of thy presence is gone. Too often we are pushed about by the cares of this world; poise and peace are far from us. We have felt the pull of thy love as it continually reaches out for us, but the adversities of life take hold upon us. When the night is dark, the storm roaring, and thy light cannot be seen nor thy voice heard, may our faith be so grounded that nothing can shake us from following thy will. O Father, grant that it may ever be so. In Jesus' name we pray. Amen.

For Those Who Are Bereaved

O Thou eternal One, Father and comforter of all men, draw especially near unto us as our hearts are filled with sadness over the loss of our loved one. What a vacancy has been left! What a heaviness has gripped our souls! What a loneliness has come upon us! If we cry, it is but natural, for thy Son too wept over his departed friend. But beyond our tears help us to know there is life that shall never end. In our sadness make us to know that thou dost understand. In our loneliness make us conscious of thy great love. In our grief draw us closer unto thee. Help us to stand bravely the anguish of these hours. Fill the vacancy of our hearts with thy abiding presence which links us to those who pass beyond. Grant that we may rest our fears in thy hands, trusting in thy promises, and waiting for the day when we shall be joined together in thy eternal home, through Jesus Christ our Lord. AMEN.

For Patience

O God, forgive us for letting life's annoyances cripple our spirits. Unexpected interruptions, necessary details, and the day's routine have marred our dispositions. To cover up our own weaknesses we have blamed them on others. To find release from explosions within we have said things we should not have said. To give expression to our impatience we have turned our anger loose upon objects nearby. For our loss of control we are deeply repentant; for our lack of inner steadiness we ask pardon. Fill us with a portion of thy ever-flowing patience and grant a new chance to redeem our unworthiness. Blow within our souls calmness sufficient for life's unrest. In the face of circumstances irritating to all of us give control, through Jesus Christ our Lord. AMEN.

For the Needy

Eternal God, who art concerned with all thy children, and whose purposes for our lives are always good, in our gratitude for the favors thou dost send our way, let us not be unmindful of the needs of others.

Give us concerned hearts for the hungry, the homeless;

Help us to remember the sick, the suffering;

Out of our bounty move us to give to the needy;

In our comfort stir us to share with the burdened;

Use us to bring cheer to little children;

Through us send hope to the discouraged.

Be especially near to those to whom the light of day brings less joy than to ourselves. Mid all the rush and strain of daily life, grant that we may pause and remember that it is more blessed to give than to receive. AMEN.

For Courage

Staunch Friend of humanity, creator of life, ruler of the universe, we come to thee seeking courage. Grant that as servants of thine we may have strength—

To stand against the crowd for what is right;

To defend, though we be misunderstood, causes of justice;

To love, in spite of racial hatred, thy children of all colors;

To speak for truth, when it is so much easier to be silent;

To oppose, though our position be endangered, those who would harm thy kingdom.

O Father, in days like these we so desperately need courage to love, to help, to lift humanity; courage to befriend those who have been cast out; courage to face life unafraid, resting on thy strength and power. Grant that it may ever be so, through Jesus Christ our Lord. Amen.

For Him Who Wants to Learn

O God, the author of all wisdom, the fountain of all truth, for him denied the privilege of schooling in early days who now late in life wants to learn, we pray at this time. So much of thy world's splendor has been shut from his gaze; books with their storehouse of knowledge and beauty have been locked to his unlettered mind; understanding of life's complex problems has been foreign to his nature. But we are grateful that thy love still tugs at his heart, and thy wisdom still pulls at his mind. Though his reading is scant and his grammar is poor, yet he can know thy care and fatherly goodness, and can walk in thy holy way. Continue to lure his mind with truth, and give him help as he enters the world of thought. Let him not be discouraged before truth too advanced for his untutored past, but challenged and more determined to uncover the riches of thy wisdom. Give to him progress in the search, and may his life in its remaining years shed light upon the pathway of others. Grant unto him an assurance that it is never too late to learn and that in life's common things are treasures of true wisdom. In the name of Christ we pray. AMEN.

To Live as Neighbors

Eternal God, into whose presence we come this day, and by whose power and grace we live, we thank thee for these moments of quietness wherein we may be still and know that thou art God. From the rush and hurry of daily life we pause to acknowledge thee as the Lord of life, and to seek from thee help for the days ahead.

Here we come as the church at worship, seeking thy face, and listening for thy voice, and hearing thy word. We need thee, O God, to help us out where we live, and to strengthen us in doing thy will in the workaday world. Grant that when we scatter, we may carry thy word of reconciliation and peace to a needy world.

Help us to be kind with those we meet, to recognize all men as children of thine. Keep us pure when we are tempted to be cowardly. Hold our tongues when we would speak ill of anyone. Give us faith and trust and love that will drive out fear and anxiety. Hold us in thy hand and help us know that in thee is our greatest assurance. In Christ's name we pray. AMEN.

For Power to Face Life

O Thou eternal God, we come into thy holy presence today lifting our careworn hearts unto thee. We know that thou art here. We feel the healing and cleansing power of thy Spirit. We want to be still and to know that thou art God.

Some of us are facing temptations that would trip us, needing thy help in withstanding them.

Some of us are lonely, missing those we have loved long since and lost awhile. We come asking for companionship.

Some of us are being ambushed by a crippling disease, needing thy assurance and the power to face it.

All of us are confronted daily with little temptations which would make us sin. We come asking for salvation from sin through Christ our Lord.

Take us up into thine arms today and make us know that thy love is sufficient for our every need.

Be with all who are suffering and in distress. Give power to the forces of right and strength to the arm of righteousness. Through Jesus Christ our Lord. AMEN.

For Guidance

O God, who bestowest thy mercy at all times on them that love thee, and in no place art distant from those that serve thee, quicken within us a sense of thy holy presence.

We come this day confessing that we have not loved thee as we ought to have loved thee; we have done those things which we ought not to have done, and we have left undone those things which should have been done. From our lips unkind words have been hastily spoken; in our minds unhealthy thoughts have been entertained; with our feet we have often followed paths of unrighteous living; with our hands we have given ourselves to unworthy tasks.

Call us back, we pray, to righteous living and to a closer walk with thee. Send us out as worthy witnesses for thee and as ambassadors of Christ our King. AMEN.

For Those Who Are Ill

O God our Father, we would quiet our souls in thy presence and rest ourselves in the confidence of thy sustaining strength, that the peace of God which passeth all understanding may guard our hearts and thoughts.

Through countless channels thou dost seek our lives; at many a door thou dost stand and knock. We wait now for thy still, small voice which can change our fear to faith and our cowardice to courage.

Grant to us faith in thee, that in the face of life's illnesses and trials we may share Jesus' trustful, confident mind, and be freed from the cares which destroy us. Grant us his unfaltering belief in thy goodness, that, whether pain or joy be our lot, we may still know ourselves to be upheld by thy strength. In his name we pray. AMEN.

For Divine Direction

Eternal God, into whose presence we come, and by whose power and grace we live, this is the day that thou hast made; help us to be joyous in it.

We confess our lack of faith and trust—
Our cowardice in the face of danger;
Our weakness in confronting temptations;
Our timidity in the presence of evil; and
Our indifference before thy claims upon us.

Lift us, we pray—
To higher levels of thinking and living;
To new insights of truth and goodness;
To new hopes and dreams of a better life;
To new strength in facing the demands of living.

Save us from weak resignation to the evils we deplore, and set our feet upon foundations whose builder and maker is God. We wait before thee, assured that thou knowest best what is good for us to do and to dare. Make known thy way and give us the will and grace to walk therein. AMEN.

For Faithfulness in Discipleship

Eternal God, once again we come into thy presence to lift our hearts in praise to thee. We know that in thee we live and move and have our being. It is thou, O God, the uncreated One, who hast created us. It is thou who dost hold within thy hand the slender thread of life.

We thank thee that thou hast given to us these days of our earthly pilgrimage and hast a place and a purpose for each of us. We are grateful to believe that thou hast called us to serve thee in faithfulness and in dedication. We do not know what each day will bring forth, but we do know him whom we have believed, and we are willing to trust each day to him. Give us a sense of thy gracious presence as we live day by day, through Jesus Christ our Lord. AMEN.

For Steadfastness

Eternal God, Father of our Lord Jesus Christ, and our Father, before the world was formed thou wert Ruler, and long after it has perished thou wilt be Ruler still. Hear us this day and speak to our feeble hearts. In a hurried world we pause; out of a sense of need we open our hearts unto thee. Look deeply within us, we pray, and drive out all that spoils, all that cankers life.

Fill us with a portion of—
Thy love which knows no barrier;
Thy courage which knows no fear;
Thy mercy ever ready to forgive;
Thy patience always seeing men's best beneath their worst;
Thy compassion which shares the cares of burdened men;
Thy wisdom which has purpose in life's ways;
Thy goodness always wanting to give us the best;
Thy beauty reflected in nature's loveliness.

Call forth the best we have to give, and grant that our wills may accept the call, through Jesus Christ our Lord we pray. AMEN.

For Freedom from Anxiety

O Thou eternal God, whose heart is filled with goodness and love for all men, whose compassion can comfort the soul in our moments of anxiety, draw us near to thee as the sun lifts the waters from the sea. Heartaches cause us to stumble, but thou art an ever-present God, whose will is to strengthen our weakness. Let not fear, trouble, or pain lessen our devotion to thee, but rather cause us to lift our eyes unto the hills from whence cometh our help. Gird us with endurance when even to exist at all requires strength not our own. Help us to realize that even in suffering thou canst use us as thou didst use the suffering of thy Son to heal a broken world. Even when life seems to be slipping away, give us a consciousness of thy presence and a realization that, though the body may break, thy love and constant care can never be taken from us. Speak to us in the lonely hours of the night when sleep will not come, and stay thou with us in the day even when clouds hang low, through Jesus Christ our Lord. AMEN.

For Trust

O Thou eternal God, who remainest the same though all else fades, who changest not with our changing moods, who leavest us not when we leave thee, we open our minds and our hearts unto thee.

With gratitude we turn our thoughts toward thy mercy and love made known in so many ways. We know that thou art with us and blessing us even when we are unaware of thy presence. We are confident that thou dost will for our lives all that is good. We are assured through Christ our Lord that thou dost go with us in all life's experiences and that the very hairs of our heads are numbered.

We are thankful for the promptings of thy Spirit. We know that thou dost seek our loyalty and dost will that we give ourselves in devotion to thee. Grant that we may open our hearts to thy Spirit and find the joy that comes in dedication to thee. Give to us a deeper and firmer hold upon thy love made manifest in the sacrifices of our Lord in his crucifixion. In the light of his love may we find our way, through Jesus Christ our Lord. AMEN.

For Everyday Tasks

O gracious Father, thou who changest not though all else changeth, thou who art the same today, yesterday, and forever, enter our hearts as we gather as a group of thy children who face a world of change. When so much is calling for our time and energy, guide our choices that we may choose wisely. Let us not give our lives to incidentals but save them for essentials. When we are tempted to forget thee, stab us awake to our dependence upon thee.

Forbid that we should be so concerned with life's details that we forget life's major interest—communion and fellowship with thee. Be with parents as they guide young life into maturity; give patience to those who work with irresponsible people; guard those who face danger; comfort those whose hearts are saddened by illness and death; give courage to us all as we meet life's uncertainties. In the name of Christ who faced life with confidence we pray. AMEN.

For Quiet Confidence

O Thou eternal God, Father of all mankind, in the midst of the rush and hurry of life we pause in thy presence to get our bearings. In thee do we find our way in life, and through thee our strength for life. Change and decay all around we see, but life's changelessness we find in thee.

Here in this place today drive out, we pray, all fear of what the future may bring. Take from us the strain and stress, and let our ordered lives confess the beauty of thy peace. Prepare us in body, mind, and soul for life's unexpectedness. Set our feet upon foundations whose builder and maker is God. Help us to know that all things work together for good to them that love thee. Grant that we may discover how the sorrows and pains of life can be used for good. Bind up our worries and heartaches with thy tender love and touch. Speak to us words of comfort and of courage.

Send us forth this day strengthened by thy Spirit with might in the inner man. Through him who is always standing by, the same Jesus Christ our Lord. AMEN.

For Faith

O eternal God, our Father, thou who hast planted hope and faith within the human breast, forgive us if the pressure of everyday life and the indifference of men cause us to waver in our labors for thee. Grant that our eyes may be lifted above and beyond the horizon of this life into the eternal, so that our perspective may be large enough for the task. Keep ever before us a consciousness of the eternities so that the present may have more meaning. Renew within us a faith in men; and empower us with a spirit which will call out the best in men. Let us never lose sight of the Light of the world; may we keep him ever close to us in our daily labors. In his name we pray. AMEN.

For Faithful Stewardship

O holy One, everlasting Father, eternal God, for this life given us we are grateful. As we live the days of our years, help us to remember our living in light of life's end. Grant that we may realize that these are but fleeting days, that our sojourn here is but a brief glimpse of this life, and knowing this may we live life to the full. But guests are we only for a little while. Help us to be considerate ones. When we pass from the scene into that other world, grant that what we leave behind may be better than what we found, and what we received may be passed on, when we leave, more fashioned to thy will. Let us never lose sight of the end as we face the present. Keep ever before us a vision of thy kingdom's goal, through Jesus Christ our Lord. Amen.

For Strength in Face of Temptations

O God, our lives are as open books to thy understanding. Forgive us, we pray, for our misdeeds. We are not asking that thou wilt free us from the pains of our sins or the wages that they surely bring, but that thou wilt give us another chance and the strength to withstand the temptations encompassing our daily lives. Give us the courage to confess our sins and the willingness to make amends for the wrong we have done.

Grant that our experiences may make us know that in our own strength we cannot overcome the temptations of life, but only as we live daily within thy presence, and draw goodness from thee who art the source of all goodness—only so can we live victoriously. In Christ's name we pray. AMEN.

For Freedom from Fear

O merciful God, companion of men's souls, strength of men's wills, comforter of men's sorrows, what would we do without thee! O gracious One—

When we are lonely, thou art near;

When we are afraid, thou dost reassure us;

When we are tempted, thou dost reinforce us;

When we are in far places, thou dost unite us in spirit with those we love;

When men fail us, thou dost hold our faith in what they can become;

When anxiety grips our inmost being, thou dost bring inner peace and calm;

When we flee from thee in sinful living, thou dost still tug at our hearts;

When we come back to thee, thou dost open thine arms in forgiveness and receive us back unto thyself again;

When life's end stares us in the face, thou art One who dost open the door into thy eternal home.

For thy presence, thy comfort, thy strength, thy power, thy forgiveness, we give thee our heart's gratitude. In the name of him who is our Lord we pray. AMEN.

For Assurance

Eternal God, creator of all life, ruler of all nature, source of all strength, we give thanks unto thee for thy great love toward us and toward all men. Into thy holy presence we come, lifting our common supplications unto thee. Thou knowest the needs of our hearts—our fears, our anxieties, our unanswered perplexities. The burdens we carry are known by thee. The heartaches which disturb us are not foreign to thy knowledge.

Keep us still that we may listen.

Keep us believing that we may know.

Keep us pure that we may see.

Keep us brave that we may venture.

Keep us close that we may walk in confidence.

Send us out, O God, with assurance that life with all its fears can be faced in victory with thee. AMEN.

For Courage in Face of Uncertainty

Eternal God, thou who hast loved us into life and dost love us through life into life eternal, once again we pause seeking thy ear and listening for thy voice.

We are continually overwhelmed at thy majesty and greatness and yet humbled in gratitude for thy personal concern in our lives. Nothing escapes thy notice, nor is foreign to thy understanding. Thou dost listen, as a father to a child, to our every prayer. Every detail of our lives is of interest to thee. What would we do, O God, without thy love, without thy courage, without thy strength, without thy comfort?

Steady those who are faced with uncertainty. Awaken those who find life drab and colorless. Give us courage to stand for truth, to say no when it is so easy to say yes, to be true to the highest we know. Help us to walk as children of thine. In Christ's name we pray. AMEN.

For the Needs of Others

Eternal God, who art concerned with all thy children and whose purposes for our lives are always good, in our gratitude for the favors thou dost send our way, let us not be unmindful of the needs of others.

Give us concerned hearts for the hungry, the sick, the suffering.

Out of our bounty move us to give to the needy.

In our comfort stir us to share with the burdened.

Use us to bring cheer to little children.

Through us send hope to the discouraged.

We would pray, O God, this day—

For the sick of body and the weary of mind;

For those weighted down with the guilt of sin;

For all who are living in fear and anxiety; and

For the sorrowful who listen for steps which will never return.

Give to all weary travelers today strength for the road ahead. In the name of him who came to help men carry life's loads we pray. AMEN.

For *Guidance of the Holy Spirit*

Eternal God, from whom cometh every good and perfect gift, we praise thee, we worship thee, we give thanks unto thee for thy great love which is constant and whose concern encompasses all men. On every hand thou dost seek to make thyself known unto us. Open our minds and hearts to thy companionship. Free us from our occupation with the cares of this world and the call of the marketplace, that we may hear thy still, small voice.

Breathe into our disordered lives a portion of thy peace.

Reassure us of thy love as we face the uncertainties of tomorrow.

Undergird us with thy strength as we walk our feeble ways.

Lighten our pathway with thy truth as we face difficult decisions.

Inspire us with thy presence and make us know we labor not alone.

Send us out with the power to do thy will, through Jesus Christ our Lord. AMEN.

For a Right Spirit

O Thou eternal God, in whom we live and move and have our being; to thee we owe life and the chance to live the days of our years. We give thee our gratitude for the privilege of living in this thy world.

We want, our Father, to give ourselves to that which makes for the good life. We know that thy way is the only way for man to live. Thou hast made known to us through Jesus Christ thy purpose for life. He is the Way, the Truth, and the Life.

But sometimes in the mad struggle to get ahead we have forgotten thee and thy way. We have been too intent upon making a living rather than making a life. We have let our greed separate us from thee. We have wandered from thy pathway.

O God, call us back to the dreams of our earlier years. Set our feet again upon the highway of God. Help us to seek first the kingdom of God and his righteousness, and all these things will be added unto us.

Take and use us for thy purposes, in Christ's name we pray. AMEN.

That Our Choices May Be Wise

O God, creator and sustainer of thy world; into our hands has been placed material out of which life is to be fashioned. With thy guidance our lives can become works of art. Grant unto us an understanding of what it is thou hast for us to do. When we are tempted to follow the selfish desires of our hearts, do thou draw us back upon the course. When choices become difficult, empower us with wisdom and insight so that we may not miss the way. Give unto us a consciousness of thy companionship, and may we find thee always a source from which strength may be drawn. In Christ's name we pray. AMEN.

For Truth and Power

Eternal God, in whom we live and move and have our being, help us to be still and know that thou art God, that in quietness and in confidence shall be our strength.

Once again we pause in thy presence seeking thy ear and listening for thy voice. We need thy truth and thy power as we move among the things of this world. It is so easy for us to forget thee and the things that belong to our peace. Daily we are tempted to live beneath the dignity that thou hast given to man, to fall short of the ideals which we know to be right and true. Forgive us for our sins and restore us to thy fellowship.

Be with those this day who are ill. Help them to know that thou art the Great Physician in whose power and providence healing takes place.

Forgive us for our broken vows of loyalty which first were spoken as we were made members of the church of Christ. Renew within us our earlier dedication and restore us to a closer walk with thee. Through Christ our Lord and in his name we pray. AMEN.

For Wisdom in Making Decisions

O God, thou hast given us another day to worship thee. Make this, we pray, a hallowed hour. We know thou art incomprehensible in thy mysterious greatness, and yet dost reveal thyself to us in so many ways. We would be still now and listen to thy voice as thou dost speak to us. We come assured that thou art ready to meet us at our point of deepest need.

There are decisions to be made which affect not only our lives but the lives of others. There are commitments that have to be made, to make more of life than now we are doing. There are chains of sins which need to be broken by the power of thy love. We need to start afresh and leave behind old ways of living.

Help us this day to be dissatisfied with ourselves, with the thoughts we are thinking, with the deeds we are doing, with the life we are living. Help us to know that we can be better than we are. Help us to be pleasant with those around us, to be willing to take our share of the load, to bear with fortitude the trials that come our way. Help us to lose ourselves in the work thou hast given us to do.

Give us the desire to be about "the Father's business," and the strength and will to do it. Amen.

For Courage to Stand for Truth

O God, in whose love we learn the meaning of life, and through whose strength we bear its burden and cross, give us the courage to stand for truth and righteousness even if it requires cost to ourselves. Grant that people may know what it means to sacrifice when they look at our lives, that they may understand the meaning of Jesus' command to return good for evil, to do good to those who hate you. Help us so to love that men may see some reflection of thy unending love for all men. Grant that by our lives we may bear witness to our faith that any man who trusts in Christ becomes a new creature. Give to us, we pray, the consciousness of thy Holy Spirit which guides us and empowers us and strengthens us. Send us forth to live at our best, through Jesus Christ our Lord. AMEN.

In Humility

Almighty God, our Father, who hast promised that where two or three are gathered together in thy name thou wilt be in the midst of them, help us, we pray, to feel thy presence in this place. Thou hast assured us that thou wilt have mercy on us and pardon our sins if only we come to thee in the spirit of humility. We come before thee asking that thou wilt help us start over again. Though we come with broken purposes of good and idle endeavors against evil, help us to do better. Purge our hearts of evil thoughts and hard feelings toward those who differ with us, and grant us thy spirit of love which was in thy Son, our Lord.

Comfort those in difficult places of decision, and give insight and wisdom to those in authority. Grant us boldness to face clouded situations and faith to trust all truth. Hear us, O God, as we lift our hearts to thee, for we need thy power and the healing of thy peace, through Jesus Christ our Lord. AMEN.

For Strength to Do Right

O Thou eternal God, who hast given us the breath of life and who hast ordained that we should be useful in thy kingdom's building, help us to see afresh thy way and thy purpose for our lives.

What we want is to do thy will and to fulfill thy plan. Grant that the lure of the marketplace and the temptations that daily confront us may not steer us from that course. We know that thy plan and thy will are best for us. But sometimes it is so hard for us to follow them. So, here today we are asking for strength to do the right and insight into what it is.

We are thankful that thou dost not expect the impossible from us, but only that we do the best we can with what we have. Help us begin now to start being our best.

We praise thee, we worship thee, we glorify thee who art for ever and ever. AMEN.

For Power to Make Us Strong

O most merciful and righteous God, into thy holy presence we come this day with praise upon our lips and thanksgiving in our hearts. Through countless ages thou hast ruled this thy world. In every generation thou art concerned in it still.

Here in this place we feel thy presence near, and we open our minds and hearts to the leadership of thy Spirit. Some of us, our Father, are weaker than others, but all of us need thy power and thy strength to make us strong. The temptations which daily confront us try our spirits. We find ourselves doing those things which we ought not to do and leaving undone those things which we ought to do. Take us this day and make us worthy servants of thine. In Christ's name we pray. AMEN.

For Comfort in Sorrow

O Thou eternal One, Father and Comforter of all men, draw especially near to all whose hearts are filled with sadness over the loss of a loved one. Beyond their tears help them to know there is life that shall never end. In their sadness help them know that thou dost understand. In their loneliness make them conscious of thy great love. In their grief draw them closer unto thee.

Help them to bear bravely the anguish of these hours. Fill the vacancy of their hearts with thy abiding presence, which links us to those who pass beyond. Grant that we may rest our fears in thy hands, trusting in thy promises and waiting for the day when we shall be joined together in thy eternal home, through Jesus Christ our Lord. AMEN.

To Be Freed from Pride

O Thou eternal God, in whom we live and move and have our being, with thankful hearts we praise thy holy name.

This is thy world, and we are thy children living in the Father's house. But we bow before thee in shame because we have not lived as kindred one with another. Our selfishness and pride have separated us, our prejudice has divided us. We have not loved one another as thou hast willed that we should. Forgive us for our unbrotherly ways.

We come, too, confessing our sin in thinking too highly of ourselves. We know that we are weak and frail beings in great need of a Redeemer and Savior who can lift us out of our sordid selves. We have done those things which we ought not to have done and left undone those things which we ought to have done.

So, we come to thee in need of the Christ who is the Savior of the world and who alone can save us from sin. Take us this day and make us more worthy servants of thine, through Jesus Christ our Lord we pray. AMEN.

For Help in Our Problems

Eternal God, into thy holy presence we come lifting our common supplications unto thee. Thou knowest the needs of our hearts, our fears, our anxieties, our unanswered perplexities. The burdens we carry are known by thee. The heartaches which disturb us are not foreign to thy knowledge.

Many of us, our Father, are heavy laden with problems too great to bear. Some of us face illness. And some of us are confronted with decisions in which thy guidance is sorely needed. We know not where to turn but to thee, remembering thy invitation, "Come unto me, all ye that labour and are heavy laden, and I will give you rest." Speak to our needs this day as we seek to open our hearts unto thee. In Christ's name we pray. AMEN.

For Humility in Face of Success

Eternal God, we lift our hearts unto thee this day as children to a common Father. Look down upon us and bind us together in concord and peace. Help us in our varied ways to find thee, and in finding thee to love thee, and in loving thee to serve thee, whom to serve is perfect freedom. Strengthen us that we may move against the paganism of today. Help us to live and serve together as brothers with one Father.

O God, grant that no success will come to our lives which would make us trust in our own strength. But let us ever feel our dependence upon thee. Give us the joy in a job well done, but let it not become an unpardonable pride of achievement. Forbid that the plaudits of men should bring to us a false sense of importance. May no material achievement lessen our devotion to thee. Rather keep us humble and make us to know that all we are and have we owe to thy boundless goodness. Give us concern that we please thee and not the voices of the world. In Christ's name we pray. AMEN.

For Freedom from Doubt

Eternal God, in whom we live and move and have our being; thou who hast loved us into life and dost love us through life into life eternal; once again we pause, seeking thy ear and listening for thy voice.

We are continually overwhelmed at thy majesty and greatness, and yet humbled in gratitude for thy personal concern in our lives. We praise thy name for the constancy of thy care and love. We can never flee from thy love wherever we are, nor escape the stern judgments of thy will whatever the sin may be. Nothing escapes thy notice, nor is foreign to thy understanding. Thou dost listen as father to child to our every prayer. Every detail of our lives is of interest to thee. What would we do, O God, without thy love, without thy courage, without thy strength, without thy comfort?

Help us, we pray, to place more dependence upon thy power and thy strength. Forgive us for resting solely upon the fragile, temporary powers of our own natures, but grant that we may turn to thee and find that strength which comes from the source of all strength, through Jesus Christ our Lord. AMEN.

For Our Families and Others Who Serve Us

For Our Homes

Dear God, who art the Father of us all, and who hast established the homes of our world, we lift our hearts unto thee in praise of mothers and fathers. May this day be a day of special gratitude for our parents, and a time when we shall do honor to them.

As children, help us to be worthy of their love and faithful to their trust in us. Forbid that we should ever forget their kindness to us and sacrifice for us. Grant that the lives we live may reflect praise upon their love and devotion to us.

And to all parents give the true sense of their mission and place in life. Help them to be noble and true, pure and loving, reflecting thy mercy and goodness to us all.

In the name of Jesus Christ our Lord we pray. AMEN.

For Our Mothers

Eternal God, we lift up our hearts in adoration. Thou hast made us one in our desire for thy fellowship, so we wait for thee to bless us with the benediction of thy presence. We thank thee that through thy nature thou dost make thyself known to us, and we would be more sensitive to thy presence. We would recognize all objects of beauty as thy handiwork. Help us to know that wherever we scatter beauty and loveliness, we remind men of thee. Give to each of us, like a scented flower, a fragrance of spirit which will add joy to life and make for contentment.

We thank thee this day for our mothers, whose gentleness and kindness brought warmth to our lives. We praise thee for the beautiful memories which cling about their lives, and for their faith in us which has given us confidence in ourselves and in thee. Help us so to live that we may do honor to their names.

Cleanse our hearts and hands that we may ascend to thy holy hill. We join our hearts together in gratitude for the gift of Jesus Christ, who has shown us the way to richer, fuller, happier lives. In his name we pray. AMEN.

For Our Mates

O God, thou who hast drawn us together as husband and wife and declared that we are one, grant that the days of our years may find us increasingly bound closer together. Keep us ever thoughtful of one another so that we may never take for granted the "little, nameless, unremembered acts of kindness and of love." In life's sorrows as well as its joys may our hearts beat as one. Help us to keep the ecstasy of courtship ever aglow in the midst of life's routine. Open our eyes to see in the depths of our growing love some reflection of thy love for us, and may our affection for each other be bound together by a higher affection for thee, for only in such can these earthly companionships withstand life's uncertainties and vicissitudes. In thy name, to whom we both bow our heads, we pray. AMEN.

A Prayer of Parents of a Newborn Babe

O eternal God, creator of all things, ruler of all nature, sustainer of all life, our hearts are filled to overflowing with joy for this newborn babe. Gratefully we acknowledge with thanksgiving the share in creation thou hast given us. In this thou hast drawn us closer unto thee, for we share thy guardianship as earthly parents praying that thou wilt give us wisdom and understanding in its fulfillment. Deeply we feel the need of thy strength and guidance in leading this little life committed to our care. May it see in us the reflection of thy fatherly goodness and learn from us thy holy ways, through Jesus Christ our Lord. AMEN.

For a Baby

O God, creator of life, architect of men's souls, for the life of this baby we give thee praise and thanksgiving. It has come to us a little bundle of capacity with all its days stretching before it. For its life thou hast a plan. For those who direct it, thou dost offer a share in the plan. Hidden within thy wisdom are possibilities for its future. Known only unto thee is its potentiality. Forbid that we who lead it should fail to offer the best. Grant that the world in which it is to grow will increasingly become an atmosphere wherein its life can reach its true fulfillment. Stay thou close to this babe as its personality unfolds, and may its life reflect thy fatherly goodness and its days be filled with thy holy ways, in the name of the Christ child we pray. AMEN.

For a Little Boy

O God, forgive me for my impatience with my little boy. He is so young, has been here so short a time, and yet I have looked upon him as an adult. I have expected him to look at life as I do, to see through eyes open for only three years as one would see through eyes which have witnessed many seasons come and go. Forgive me for my lack of appreciation that thou hast made life to grow—first the seed, then the blade, and then the full ear of corn. As with nature so with thy children thou hast ordained it. Use me as a parent who understands and seeks to lead in every stage of his life's pilgrimage, through Jesus Christ our Lord. AMEN.

For Nurses

Eternal God, in whom we live and move and have our being, we give thee our gratitude for life's healing powers. We know that as thou hast made us, it is within thy power to restore life when in need of repair.

We are thankful for all thy servants who do thy bidding in ministering to the broken bodies of men. Especially are we grateful for the tender concern, the skilled hands, and trained minds of nurses, who give of themselves in dedicated service.

Grant unto them a portion of thy strength and a measure of thy compassion as they bind up the wounds of suffering humanity. Give them patience in facing unreasonable demands, and endurance for the long hours of toil. May theirs be joyful hearts in seeing their tasks as part of thy plan in serving the needs of mankind.

Through Jesus Christ our Lord. AMEN.

For Leaders in the Church

O God, when our service to this church is over and its care passes into other hands, grant that we may not leave it heartless or spiritually weak. Forbid that our selfish desires should rob it of leadership which is virile. Give us courage to stand for truth, righteousness, and justice, even if it requires great cost to ourselves. Let our people see what it means to sacrifice when they look at our lives; to know what Jesus was talking about when he said return good for evil, do good to those who hate you. Help them to understand what it is to forgive, and to catch a glimpse of thy unending love for lost humanity when they see our love brooding over their sins. O Father, to leave thy church more spiritually awake than we found it requires strength not our own, wisdom that cometh from thee. Drive us as leaders to our knees, and keep ever before us thy matchless love, through Jesus Christ our Lord. AMEN.

For Those in a Healing Ministry

Eternal God, in whom there is no darkness, and from whom we find light for life's journey, thou art great in power, unlimited in wisdom, and infinite in all the resources of thy being.

We thank thee for the heritage that is ours, for the dreams and ideals which have been handed down to us, for the fearless courage which has caused man to go in relentless search of the enemies of human welfare, and for all movements and institutions which make for better living.

We are grateful for the generosity of many who have given of their substance that institutions of healing may bring aid to the sick in mind and body; for doctors and scientists whose long years of study bring a healing ministry to those in distress; for the tender concern of nurses who give of themselves in dedicated service; and for all who walk beside those who would heal. In Christ's name we pray. AMEN.

A Prayer of Teachers

O Thou eternal spirit of truth, beauty, and goodness, thou art greater than our minds can conceive thee to be. Thy majesty and power are beyond our keenest imaginations, and yet we must presume to speak thy mind and know thy heart. As teachers we endeavor to tell men who thou art and what thou wouldst have them do. We speak in thy name and for thy sake. Yet, our Father, we come to thee so seldom and remain with thee so short a time to hear and to know what thou wouldst have us say. Thou art continually knocking at our doors, but life's demands shut thee out and we do not open the door. Forgive us for our negligence, shame us for our assumptions, and grant us the power, poise, and peace that come only from thee, and which can be passed on only as we receive them in communion with thee. Free us from ourselves, purge us from bitterness, hatred, jealousy, envy, and make us fit servants of thine. Through Jesus Christ our Lord. AMEN.

For Friends Who Believe in Us

O God, for kind friends and associates who believe in us we are thankful. We know full well that our efforts are poor, and the results often meager; yet a kind word or an encouraging smile sends people on their way determined to be faithful to their trust. For these friends, who see the good beneath our rough exterior and whose faith brings it forth, our hearts are deeply grateful. Above all, our Father, we thank thee for thy faith in us revealed through Christ our Lord; and in his name we pray. AMEN.

For Our State and Nation

Eternal God, in whom there is no darkness and from whom we find light for life's journey, we thank thee for the communities in which we live and for all institutions which make for better living.

We thank thee for the heritage that is ours; for the dreams and ideals which have been handed down to us; for this our native land and our priceless treasures of freedom; and for the faith of our fathers living still.

We pray especially this day for our state and nation and for all influences which make for better government. We thank thee for patriotic men and women who give of themselves in public service, and whose self-interest gives way to public welfare.

Guard those who patrol our streets and keep watch for fires;

Give strength to the arm of law;

Give wisdom to those who sit in judgment;

Give insight to those who make decisions;

Give courage to those who stand for the right;

Give concern to those who are governed; and

Give us wisdom, give us courage, for the facing of these days, through Jesus Christ our Lord. AMEN.

For Special Days and Seasons

For the New Year

Almighty and everlasting God, in whom we live and move and have our being, thou hast been our dwelling place in all generations. Before the mountains were brought forth, or ever thou hadst formed the earth and the world, even from everlasting to everlasting, thou art God.

We come with hearts grateful for thy care and goodness during the days passed. We thank thee for thy guiding hand which has been ready to direct us and restrain us, for thy watchful eye which has protected us, and for thy love which has been a constant source of care for all our affairs. In our joys thou hast rejoiced. In our sorrows thou hast wept, and in our failures thou hast been concerned.

Forgive us, we pray, for time misspent in the vanished days, and bless us when we have truly striven to do thy will. Help us to improve upon whatever future thou dost stretch out before us. Impart to us good resolutions, and give us the will and strength to keep them. Remind us day by day of our dependence upon thee, and help us to amend our lives according to thy holy will, through Christ our Lord. AMEN.

For Brotherhood Week

O God, who hast made of one blood all nations of men; help us to know that thou art the Father of us all and that we are brothers one to another. We thank thee that no barrier of race or clan may keep men from thee. We are all members of thy great family and need to learn from thee how to live as brothers. Thou wouldst have us live together in concord and peace. Help us who have been so favored to learn how to share, how to appreciate those who through chance are denied so much in life.

Forbid that we should harbor false pride of race or nationality, but breathe into our being a deep humility. Give us mature minds that will help us understand the crisis of men today. Give us clear vision that we may judge men by what they are and not by what group they are in.

Take us, lift us, inspire us, strengthen us, through Jesus Christ our Lord. AMEN.

For Lent

Eternal God, whose majesty and greatness are beyond the understanding of our minds, and yet whose presence is within the hearts of us all; we open our minds to the wonder of thy being and our hearts to the joy of thy companionship.

We thank thee for the world thou hast prepared for us as our dwelling place. But beyond the creation of thy hands we are filled with awe before thee as we know thee in Christ. We are overwhelmed with thy love as expressed in the cross; such suffering love commands our love in return.

During these days leading toward Easter, we remember his passion and sacrifice for sinful humanity; we remember his death and resurrection which have changed the course of history and which offer eternal life to all who believe on his name.

Grant, our Father, that we may become more worthy of such love, and during these days may we discipline ourselves to become fit channels of thy love. Take us as we are, and make us over through Christ our Lord. AMEN.

For Palm Sunday

O Thou ever-present God, whose will it is that all men shall have life abundant; speak to us now. As we gaze upon thy matchless beauty, we see our own ugly selves. As thy boundless goodness makes itself known to us, we feel the evil ways within ourselves. Receiving thy forgiveness for our misdeeds, we are confronted with our failure to forgive those who have offended us. Grant that our feebleness may be turned into strength, our failures point toward successes, and our fears be changed into courage.

Endue us with the spirit to forgive, even when it is human to seek revenge. Kindle within us a desire to do right, and undergird our weakness with thy divine strength that it may be done. Grant that as followers of thine we may care greatly about those who do not care, and may love those who do not love us, for in so doing we indeed become children of thine, through Jesus Christ our Lord. AMEN.

For Easter

Eternal God, thou who makest the stars and turnest the shadow of death into the morning, we thank thee for the resurrection of the springtime, for the everlasting hopes that rise within the human heart, and for the gospel which has brought life and immortality to light.

Prepare our minds and hearts for this blessed season; make us conscious of our sins and shortcomings. As we think of those forces which led to the crucifixion of our Lord, help us to see in ourselves the sins which led to his death. Recall to our minds the sacrifices which were his, that we may know better the height and depth of thy love.

Make us rejoice that the darkness could not hold him and that he is alive forevermore, through Jesus Christ our Lord. AMEN.

On Mother's Day

Eternal God, creator of all life, ruler of all nature, source of all strength, in whom we live and move and have our being, we give thanks unto thee for thy great love toward us and all men. On every hand we see thy love and mercy expressed.

We thank thee that thou didst place us in homes where love is and parents are. Especially are we grateful for the love of mothers, and we bless thee for our own mothers. We thank thee for their tireless labor, for their voiceless prayers, and for their faith in us even when we did not deserve it. Help us all so to live that our lives may reflect honor upon the names of our mothers and we may be worthy of their love.

Grant that the desire for permanent peace common to the hearts of all mothers may become a reality and have its beginnings in our time. Give loud voice to this cry, and may it be heard in the ears of men in whose hands the destinies of nations rest.

In the name of Christ our Lord, whose mother inspires the mothers of men today, we pray. AMEN.

On Father's Day

Eternal God, in whose world we live, and from whom we gain strength for our days, we lift our hearts to thee this day in praise and adoration. We thank thee for the heritage that is ours, for the dreams and ideals which have been handed down to us, for this our native land and our priceless treasures of freedom.

Be especially near today to all fathers upon whose shoulders rest heavy cares. Grant them strength to fulfill their tasks. Give them a clear vision of the place they hold. Help them to be true to the meaning of fatherhood as given by Christ our Lord. Guide them that they may become worthy examples for younger men to follow. Strengthen them in the face of temptation and confirm them in the faith.

Help us all to be true to the highest we know, to follow the truth as we see it, and to give ourselves into thy care and keeping, through Jesus Christ our Lord. AMEN.

For Rural Life Sunday

Almighty God, who hast given us this good land for our heritage, who hast provided for us all the good things of life, forgive us for our failure to share with all men what thou dost provide.

We have made use of the resources of thy earth, have tilled the soil, hewn the forest, and produced in plenty the necessities of this life. The mind of man has mastered the machine and with it filled his barns and storehouses to overflowing. Yet, our Father, some of thy children are crying today for bread which has been burned, clothes which have been stored, fruit which has decayed, and meat which has spoiled.

We have made use of thy bounty in production, but have defied thy laws of distribution. Grant us wisdom and the will needed to make these adjustments. Empower us with love which will not rest until it is done. Give us concern, O Lord, for all thy children, who are our brothers. In the spirit of Christ we pray. AMEN.

On Labor Sunday

O God, whose Son Jesus was once carpenter at Nazareth, we pray thee for the workers of the world. Thankfully we come unto thee who hast made all worthy labor honorable, who through thy Son showed us that work with our hands is dignified. May we see in the tasks at hand our share in thy kingdom's building. Grant that our work be spiritualized, that its usefulness be given purpose, and that its drudgery give way to the fuller meaning of its ministry.

Whatever we do, O God, whether it be behind a loom, in a shop, behind a desk, over a stove, across a counter, in a field—may it all be turned to thee for sanction and direction. Send us out today with new faith and hope to be used in the building of thy great kingdom on earth, through Jesus Christ our Lord. AMEN.

On Thanksgiving Sunday

Eternal God, Father of all mercies, and God of all comfort, we lift our hearts and voices to thee this day in grateful praise.

We thank thee for the good earth yielding her fruit and grain for our sustenance. We thank thee for this our native land and our priceless treasures of freedom; for thy mercies bestowed upon this nation and the ideal of equal opportunity for all. We are grateful for the American dream that protects the rights of the minority and gives the individual a place of importance in our land.

We are grateful this Thanksgiving season for all who have given us a vision of the eternal which has lighted our path and strengthened our hearts. Especially are we grateful for the wonder and majesty of thy nature as we know thee in Christ; for thy love which will not let us go and which cannot be altered by life's changing moods. We thank thee that thou art near us even when we are unaware of thy presence; and that thy purposes for us are always good.

Give us grace to show forth thy praise, not only with our lips but in our lives, through Jesus Christ our Lord. AMEN.

For Advent

O God our Father, who didst send forth thy Son to be King of Kings and Prince of Peace, grant that this Christmas he may be born not only in our memories but anew in our hearts. Help us come to this festive season seeking him, as did the shepherds of old, that we may go home a new way—new men, new creatures in Christ.

O Lord, we stand before thee as one from whom no secrets are hid.

May thy beauty transform our ugliness.

May thy love drive out our hate.

May thy goodness penetrate our evil.

May thy mercy forgive our unworthiness.

May thy hope calm our fears.

May thy humility shame our arrogance.

May thy joy invade our sorrow.

O God, do thou mend the threadbare garment of our spirits, that the star which first pointed the way may be the light that shall lead us out of darkness, through Jesus Christ our Lord. AMEN.

For Christmas

Dear God, simply but sincerely we lift our hearts to thee, saying, "Thank you for Jesus!" We remember the first announcement of his coming, and the words that linger in our memories: "Fear not . . . good tidings . . . great joy . . . all people . . . Saviour . . . Christ the Lord."

It is a long way from Bethlehem to our homes; it is a long way from a crib in a stable to a crib in our own hearts; it is a long time since that first Christmas to this Christmas; but as new life came into the world then, it is our faith that it can come into our lives today.

We confess that—

> Though Christ a thousand times
> In Bethlehem be born,
> If He's not born in thee
> Thy soul is still forlorn.

Over the tumult of our world and the noise of the marketplace, may the voice of Christ ring clear and true, speaking the word of peace and reconciliation to our wayward ways. In his name we offer our prayer. AMEN.